Francis Frith's
DUBLIN

PHOTOGRAPHIC MEMORIES

Francis Frith's
AROUND DUBLIN

◆

Helen Livingston

FRITH
BOOK CO

Paperback edition published in the United Kingdom in 2000 by Frith Book Company Ltd

Reprinted in 2000

First published in the United Kingdom in 1999 by
Frith Book Company Ltd

British Library Cataloguing in Publication Data

Around Dublin
Helen Livingston
ISBN 1-85937-231-7

Frith Book Company Ltd
Frith's Barn, Teffont,
Salisbury, Wiltshire SP3 5QP
Tel: +44 (0) 1722 716 376
Email: info@frithbook.co.uk
www.frithbook.co.uk

Printed and bound in Great Britain

Front cover: Grafton Street 1897 39215

CONTENTS

FRANCIS FRITH: *Victorian Pioneer*

FRANCIS FRITH, Victorian founder of the world-famous photographic archive, was a complex and multitudinous man. A devout Quaker and a highly successful Victorian businessman, he was both philosophic by nature and pioneering in outlook.

By 1855 Francis Frith had already established a wholesale grocery business in Liverpool, and sold it for the astonishing sum of £200,000, which is the equivalent today of over £15,000,000. Now a multi-millionaire, he was able to indulge his passion for travel. As a child he had pored over travel books written by early explorers, and his fancy and imagination had been stirred by family holidays to the sublime mountain regions of Wales and Scotland. 'What a land of spirit-stirring and enriching scenes and places!' he had written. He was to return to these scenes of grandeur in later years to 'recapture the thousands of vivid and tender memories', but with a different purpose. Now in his thirties, and captivated by the new science of photography, Frith

set out on a series of pioneering journeys to the Nile regions that occupied him from 1856 until 1860.

INTRIGUE AND ADVENTURE

He took with him on his travels a specially-designed wicker carriage that acted as both dark-room and sleeping chamber. These far-flung journeys were packed with intrigue and adventure. In his life story, written when he was sixty-three, Frith tells of being held captive by bandits, and of fighting 'an awful midnight battle to the very point of surrender with a deadly pack of hungry, wild dogs'. Sporting flowing Arab costume, Frith arrived at Akaba by camel seventy years before Lawrence, where he encountered 'desert princes and rival sheikhs, blazing with jewel-hilted swords'.

During these extraordinary adventures he was assiduously exploring the desert regions bordering the Nile and patiently recording the antiquities and peoples with his camera. He was the first photographer to venture beyond the sixth cataract. Africa was still the mysterious 'Dark Continent', and Stanley and Livingstone's historic meeting was a decade into the future. The conditions for picture taking confound belief. He laboured for hours in his wicker dark-room in the sweltering heat of the desert, while the volatile chemicals fizzed dangerously in their trays. Often he was forced to work in remote tombs and caves where conditions were cooler. Back in London he exhibited his photographs and was 'rapturously cheered' by members of the Royal Society. His reputation as a photographer was made overnight. An eminent modern historian has likened their impact on the population of the time to that on our own generation of the first photographs taken on the surface of the moon.

VENTURE OF A LIFE-TIME

Characteristically, Frith quickly spotted the opportunity to create a new business as a specialist publisher of photographs. He lived in an era of immense and sometimes violent change. For the poor in the early part of Victoria's reign work was a drudge and the hours long, and people had precious little free time to enjoy themselves.

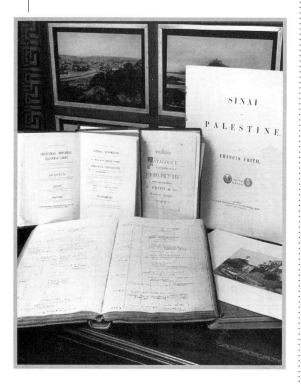

Most had no transport other than a cart or gig at their disposal, and had not travelled far beyond the boundaries of their own town or village. However, by the 1870s, the railways had threaded their way across the country, and Bank Holidays and half-day Saturdays had been made obligatory by Act of Parliament. All of a sudden the ordinary working man and his family were able to enjoy days out and see a little more of the world.

With characteristic business acumen, Francis Frith foresaw that these new tourists would enjoy having souvenirs to commemorate their days out. In 1860 he married Mary Ann Rosling and set out with the intention of photographing every city, town and village in Britain. For the next thirty years he travelled the country by train and by pony and trap, producing fine photographs of seaside resorts and beauty spots that were keenly bought by millions of Victorians. These prints were painstakingly pasted into family albums and pored over during the dark nights of winter, rekindling precious memories of summer excursions.

THE RISE OF FRITH & CO

Frith's studio was soon supplying retail shops all over the country. To meet the demand he gathered about him a small team of photographers, and published the work of independent artist-photographers of the calibre of Roger Fenton and Francis Bedford. In order to gain some understanding of the scale of Frith's business one only has to look at the catalogue issued by Frith & Co in 1886: it runs to some 670

pages, listing not only many thousands of views of the British Isles but also many photographs of most European countries, and China, Japan, the USA and Canada – note the sample page shown above from the hand-written *Frith & Co* ledgers detailing pictures taken. By 1890 Frith had created the greatest specialist photographic publishing company in the world, with over 2,000 outlets – more than the combined number that Boots and WH Smith have today! The picture on the right shows the *Frith & Co* display board at Ingleton in the Yorkshire Dales. Beautifully constructed with mahogany frame and gilt inserts, it could display up to a dozen local scenes.

POSTCARD BONANZA

The ever-popular holiday postcard we know today took many years to develop. In 1870 the Post Office issued the first plain cards, with a pre-printed stamp on one face. In 1894 they allowed other publishers' cards to be sent through the mail with an attached adhesive halfpenny stamp. Demand grew rapidly, and in 1895 a new size of postcard was permitted called the court card, but there was little room for illustration. In 1899, a year after Frith's death, a new card measuring 5.5 x 3.5 inches became the standard format, but it was not until 1902 that the divided back came into being, with address and message on one face and a full-size illustration on the other. *Frith & Co* were in the vanguard of postcard development, and Frith's sons Eustace and Cyril continued their father's monumental task, expanding the number of views offered to the public and recording more and more places in Britain, as the coasts and countryside were opened up to mass travel.

Francis Frith died in 1898 at his villa in Cannes, his great project still growing. The archive he created continued in business for another seventy years. By 1970 it contained over a third of a million pictures of 7,000 cities, towns and villages. The massive photographic record Frith has left to us stands as a living monument to a special and very remarkable man.

Frith's Archive: *A Unique Legacy*

FRANCIS FRITH'S legacy to us today is of immense significance and value, for the magnificent archive of evocative photographs he created provides a unique record of change in 7,000 cities, towns and villages throughout Britain over a century and more. Frith and his fellow studio photographers revisited locations many times down the years to update their views, compiling for us an enthralling and colourful pageant of British life and character.

We tend to think of Frith's sepia views of Britain as nostalgic, for most of us use them to conjure up memories of places in our own lives with which we have family associations. It often makes us forget that to Francis Frith they were records of daily life as it was actually being lived in the cities, towns and villages of his day. The Victorian age was one of great and often bewildering change for ordinary people, and though the pictures evoke an impression of slower times, life was as busy and hectic as it is today.

We are fortunate that Frith was a photographer of the people, dedicated to recording the minutiae of everyday life. For it is this sheer wealth of visual data, the painstaking chronicle of changes in dress, transport, street layouts, buildings, housing, engineering and landscape that captivates us so much today. His remarkable images offer us a powerful link with the past and with the lives of our ancestors.

TODAY'S TECHNOLOGY

Computers have now made it possible for Frith's many thousands of images to be accessed almost instantly. In the Frith archive today, each photograph is carefully 'digitised' then stored on a CD Rom. Frith archivists can locate a single photograph amongst thousands within seconds. Views can be catalogued and sorted under a variety of categories of place and content to the immediate benefit of researchers. Inexpensive reference prints can be created for them at the touch of a mouse button, and a wide range of books and other printed materials assembled and published for a wider, more general readership - in the next twelve months over a hundred Frith local history titles will be published! The

See Frith at www. francisfrith.co.uk

10

day-to-day workings of the archive are very different from how they were in Francis Frith's time: imagine the herculean task of sorting through eleven tons of glass negatives as Frith had to do to locate a particular sequence of pictures! Yet the archive still prides itself on maintaining the same high standards of excellence laid down by Francis Frith, including the painstaking cataloguing and indexing of every view.

It is curious to reflect on how the internet now allows researchers in America and elsewhere greater instant access to the archive than Frith himself ever enjoyed. Many thousands of individual views can be called up on screen within seconds on one of the Frith internet sites, enabling people living continents away to revisit the streets of their ancestral home town, or view places in Britain where they have enjoyed holidays. Many overseas researchers welcome the chance to view special theme selections, such as transport, sports, costume and ancient monuments.

We are certain that Francis Frith would have heartily approved of these modern developments, for he himself was always working at the very limits of Victorian photographic technology.

THE VALUE OF THE ARCHIVE TODAY

Because of the benefits brought by the computer, Frith's images are increasingly studied by social historians, by researchers into genealogy and ancestory, by architects, town planners, and by teachers and schoolchildren involved in local history projects. In addition, the archive offers every one of us a unique opportunity to examine the places where we and our families have lived and worked down the years. Immensely successful in Frith's own era, the archive is now, a century and more on, entering a new phase of popularity.

THE PAST IN TUNE WITH THE FUTURE

Historians consider the Francis Frith Collection to be of prime national importance. It is the only archive of its kind remaining in private ownership and has been valued at a million pounds. However, this figure is now rapidly increasing as digital technology enables more and more people around the world to enjoy its benefits.

Francis Frith's archive is now housed in an historic timber barn in the beautiful village of Teffont in Wiltshire. Its founder would not recognize the archive office as it is today. In place of the many thousands of dusty boxes containing glass plate negatives and an all-pervading odour of photographic chemicals, there are now ranks of computer screens. He would be amazed to watch his images travelling round the world at unimaginable speeds through network and internet lines.

The archive's future is both bright and exciting. Francis Frith, with his unshakeable belief in making photographs available to the greatest number of people, would undoubtedly approve of what is being done today with his lifetime's work. His photographs, depicting our shared past, are now bringing pleasure and enlightenment to millions around the world a century and more after his death.

DUBLIN – *An Introduction*

DUBLIN is acknowledged as one of the most lovely capital cities of Europe, celebrated for her wide tree-lined streets, graceful Georgian squares and imposing buildings fronting the River Liffey. Today she is the capital city of the Republic of Ireland, but when the photographs in this book were taken at the end of the 19th century, Dublin was under British rule and generally regarded as the second capital of the British Empire.

Dublin's history is long and complex, the very pulse of the history of Ireland itself. It was mentioned by Ptolemy in AD 140 and was visited by St Patrick in AD 448. He is said to have baptised many people at an holy well, rediscovered in 1901 near the present St Patrick's Cathedral, and there is no doubt that the Dublin area contained many early Celtic churches and monasteries. None the less, the city of Dublin itself was not founded until the arrival of Viking invaders from Scandinavia in the 9th century, when they established a defended ford and town at the Black Pool - Dubh Linn - the confluence of the Rivers Poddle and Liffey. The Vikings of Dublin intermarried with the locals and, over the next two hundred years, fought against

Danish invasions. Dublin is mentioned in the Viking sagas as an important centre and trading post. Ultimately the Danes drove the Vikings out at the Battle of Clontarf in 1014. Dublin waxed prosperous under the Danes, and was an important walled town for three centuries, until Danish power itself waned with constant attacks from the Irish, and the Anglo-Normans, under the Earl of Pembroke, appeared on the scene.

Richard de Clare, Earl of Pembroke, and commonly known as 'Strongbow', arrived in Dublin in 1170. This remarkable man married an important Irishwoman and inherited the kingdom of Leinster. Fearful that the Earl was about to set up an independent kingdom in Ireland, Henry II arrived with a substantial army and ensured that Strongbow handed over his possessions to the English crown. Thus Henry was able to proclaim himself overlord of Dublin and set up an English 'colony' in Ireland with its own parliament and exchequer. In reality the colony consisted only of the 'Pale', the few hundred square miles of land surrounding Dublin. Typically of the Normans, Strongbow, though a great warrior, was also a devoutly religious man. He set about rebuilding in stone the wooden Viking church of the Holy Trinity, now Christchurch Cathedral, and was buried there on his death in 1176 - the same year that Henry II's beloved 'Fair Rosamund' died at Godstow in Oxfordshire. Strongbow's importance as a Dublin figurehead was shown in the 16th century. His effigy in Christchurch Cathedral was broken when the south nave wall collapsed in 1569. The Lord Deputy, Sir Henry Sidney (father of the illustrious Sir Philip), hastened to install a replacement, since legal contracts frequently specified

guilds. Dublin Castle was raised on the site of the original Viking stronghold between the years 1213 and 1228, and was to remain the visible sign of British supremacy for the next seven centuries.

During the Middle Ages Dublin witnessed many historical events, including the coronation in 1437 of Lambert Simnel, pretender to the English throne, as Edward VI, supported by both the archbishop of Dublin and the Lord Deputy of Ireland. In 1534 came the famous rebellion of 'Silken' Thomas Fitzgerald, so nicknamed because of his luxu-

'Strongbow's Tomb' as a place of payment.

Dublin developed into a typical walled medieval city: overcrowded, susceptible to fire and pestilence and crowded yearly with pilgrims visiting numerous religious shrines. The chief of these were St Patrick's Cathedral with its Holy Well at which the saint himself had baptised the heathen, and Christchurch Cathedral with its famous relic the 'baccall losa' (staff of Jesus). Many feast-days and pageants brightened the year, especially the Corpus Christi pageant, in which representations of biblical stories were funded by the city

rious clothes. During the Elizabethan era there was a concerted attempt to 'civilise' Ireland causing widespread resentment and rebellion beyond Dublin, but accentuating the relative stability of life in the capital. In 1560 Ireland was proclaimed an Anglican country and Protestants took over the old churches and the two cathedrals. English settlers started to arrive anew and Dublin began to expand afresh. In 1591 Trinity College was founded, a Protestant university, on the erstwhile site of a monastery dissolved under Henry VIII in the 1530s. In this way came about the well-documented gulf between prosperous Protestant Dublin and the basically Catholic country of Ireland.

Oliver Cromwell's punitive campaigns in Ireland had little effect upon Dublin itself save to drive the well-off back into town from their newly developed suburbia. This return to the city spawned much of Dublin's great architecture, most of which was built from about 1660 - the year of Charles II's restoration to the throne. So it was that Dublin Castle was rebuilt and buildings such as the Library erected at Trinity College. In 1720 the Wide Street Commissioners oversaw the creation and development of the main thoroughfares of the city including O'Connell Street (originally Sackville Street). Indeed, architecturally, as in the arts in general, the Georgian period was one of great flowering in Dublin. Up went the superb new Parliament House (now the Bank of Ireland), opened in 1731, and up went other first-class buildings such as the Custom House and the Four Courts, as well as numerous elegant town houses.

The glittering Dublin of the Georgian era was dubbed 'this gorgeous mask of Ireland's distress', and inevitably the suppression of Catholicism bred discontent and led to violent demonstration and open rebellion. There was a growing awareness of Irish nationalism that cut across religious divides, and many Dublin Protestants spearheaded the growing nationalist movement. Legislative independence was won by Henry Grattan in 1782, and some of the worst laws repealed. None the less, the 1798 Rebellion, inspired by the French Revolution, led not to an independent Ireland but the dissolution of the Irish Parliament - said to be the only parliament in history to have voted for its own extinction - and the Act of Union with Great Britain. In 1803 Dublin witnessed Robert Emmett's unsuccessful insurrection, but the fight was continued by the lawyer Daniel O'Connell, who earned for himself the name 'The Liberator' for furthering the cause of Catholic Emancipation. He became Dublin's first Catholic Lord Mayor in 1841. O'Connell wished to turn his attention to Irish independence but was thwarted by the ravages of the potato famine which decimated Ireland's peasant population. Many starved, and some one and a half million people left the country for good, most of them sailing to America. Dublin's upper classes and intelligentsia were little affected by the potato famine, and continued in the social round and the establishment of such improving institutions as the Natural History Museum, but the city's population increased dramatically as the rural poor streamed in. Thus for the first time Dublin's Catholic population exceeded its Protestant population in considerable numbers and helped pave the way for the events of the next century.

Many Irish people were convinced of the need for total independence from Britain and the Fenian Brotherhood was formed. In the late 1870s the Fenians enlisted the help of Charles Stewart Parnell in the struggle to help Irish farmers. Parnell's powerful arguments dominated the English parliament in the 1880s and forced Gladstone to introduce the Land Acts, which enabled tenants to buy their land. Parnell then turned his attention to Home Rule for Ireland, but the bill was defeated in 1886 and soon after Parnell's career was ruined by the scandal surrounding his relationship with a married woman. He died in 1891 and was buried in Glasnevin cemetery in Dublin - the grave is pictured here. A curious incident is related concerning his funeral: as his body was lowered into the grave, the extensive funeral party saw a star fall in broad daylight. The poet Yeats, who was not actually present, wondered if it was real or a collective hallucination.

By the close of the 19th century the nationalist cause in Ireland was gathering momentum, especially in Dublin. The photographs in this book were taken in the 1890s and early 1900s, and show the city prior to the destruction wrought by the Easter Rising of 1916 and the Civil War which followed the Anglo-Irish Treaty and establishment of the Irish Free State in 1921. They show the elegant Georgian architecture, the wide streets, parks and monuments of a vanished age, where horse-drawn trams and carriages crowd the streets. At that time Dublin was the centre of a remarkable literary flowering, the Irish Literary Renaissance, led by the writings of Yeats, which inspired the founding of the Abbey Theatre in 1904 and furthered the cause of Irish nationalism. At the same time the city was the breeding ground of the Gaelic League, set up in 1893 to reintroduce Gaelic as Ireland's national language, and leading towards the Easter Rising of 1916 and ultimately to the establishment of the Irish Free State.

Famous Streets, The River Liffey and Parks

DUBLIN is renowned for her gracious Georgian streets lined by imposing buildings, and these old photographs, mostly dating from the 1890s, do justice to the subject. O'Connell Street is undoubtedly the most important street in Dublin and has witnessed several historic events. Throughout the 19th century it was known as Sackville Street but was renamed after the great nationalist leader in 1924. The most prominent of the monuments set along this wide street's central mall is a statue of O'Connell himself, facing the bridge over the River Liffey. The General Post Office stands on the west side of the Street. This was the headquarters of the rebels in the Easter Rising of 1916 and from its steps Patrick Pearse read the declaration of the Republic. The building still bears marks of the fighting. In 1922, during the Civil War, the eastern side of the street was burned down. The imposing Nelson's Pillar, prominent in these pictures, no longer stands. It was erected in 1815 to honour the victor of Trafalgar, and predated the famous London column by 32 years. It was damaged by the IRA in 1966 and had to be demolished. Its place is now taken by the Anna Livia Fountain of 1988, representing the spirit of the River Liffey and universally dubbed 'the floozy in the jacuzzi'.

South of the river are Westmoreland Street - directly south of O'Connell Bridge - College Green and Grafton Street. Westmoreland Street was created in the late 18th century as part of the scheme to run an important thoroughfare from north to south across the river. It possesses some interesting and varied architecture. College Green, once common land just south of the river, became first the home of Trinity College, built on the site of a former monastery, and later was graced by the magnificent Bank of Ireland, built originally as the Irish Parliament. It was entirely built up long before these 1890s pictures were taken, and is now a very busy traffic island, so that by comparison these photographs possess an aura of serenity. Grafton Street, a residential area in the 18th century, became a stylish shopping street over a century ago and has remained so right up to the present time. It was pedestrianised in the 1980s and is now known for its street entertainers.

Dublin possesses many parks, including two represented here, the huge Phoenix Park on the north west of the city and little St Stephen's Green on the south. The latter was originally an open common but was enclosed in 1663; later an elegant Georgian square was erected around it. In the 1880s the green was landscaped and opened to the public by Lord Ardilaun. It has always been noted for its collection of statues. Phoenix Park, which covers 1,752 acres and is eight miles in circumference, is the largest urban park in Europe. It was enclosed in 1662, when a herd of fallow deer was introduced. The park was not opened to the public until the 1740s.

Dublin is an historic port, situated on the tidal River Liffey. The port was developed from medieval times, when much of the former wide tidal estuary was reclaimed. The Liffey was embanked in 1714 and Dublin Harbour came into existence. The first quay was at North Wall. This was followed by South Wall, which starts at Ringsend, where Oliver Cromwell is said to have landed in 1649. The North and South Bull Walls were built later. The former Custom House Dock was built in 1791 at the same time as the famous Custom House. These 1890s pictures of Dublin Harbour show a vanished world of steamers, sailing ships and hard manual work.

SACKVILLE STREET 1897 39207

SACKVILLE STREET
1897 39205

At this time, O'Connell Street was still known as Sackville Street. The monument to O'Connell is in the foreground and the Nelson Monument to the right. The big Greek portico of the General Post Office of 1818 is prominent in the centre of the picture. It played a central part in the Easter Rising in 1916.

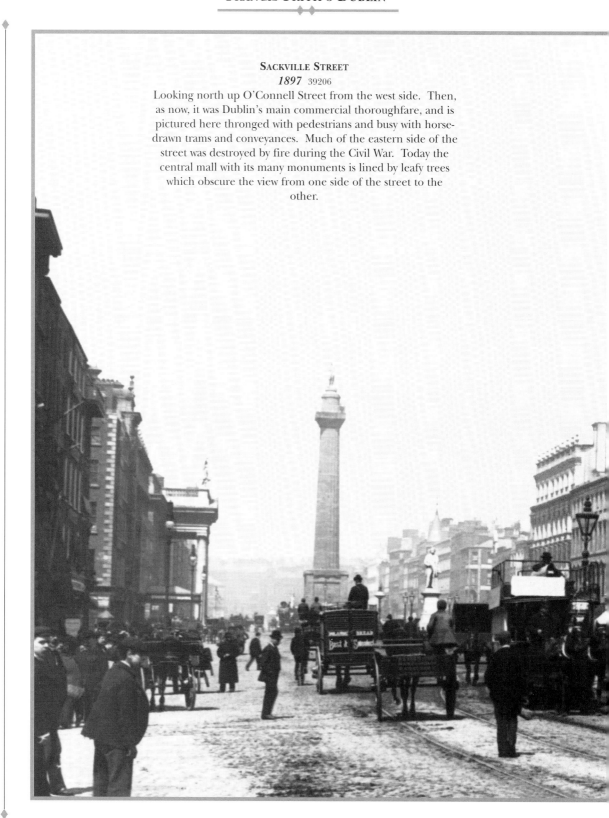

SACKVILLE STREET
1897 39206

Looking north up O'Connell Street from the west side. Then, as now, it was Dublin's main commercial thoroughfare, and is pictured here thronged with pedestrians and busy with horse-drawn trams and conveyances. Much of the eastern side of the street was destroyed by fire during the Civil War. Today the central mall with its many monuments is lined by leafy trees which obscure the view from one side of the street to the other.

SACKVILLE STREET 1897 39204

A view of O'Connell Street looking north with O'Connell Bridge over the River Liffey in the foreground. When O'Connell Bridge was built in 1790 it was known as Carlisle Bridge, and altered for ever the original concept of O'Connell Street as an elegant residential area. It became instead the city's main route from north to south.

WESTMORELAND STREET 1897 39214

An early morning scene looking south. The imposing Greek portico is the east front of the Bank of Ireland, originally the entrance to the House of Lords of the Irish Parliament, erected by James Gandon in 1785.

GRAFTON STREET 1897 39215
Looking north along Grafton Street towards Trinity College and the east portico of the Bank of Ireland. Grafton Street is Dublin's most elegant shopping street. Today it is pedestrianised, but a century ago it was full of horse-drawn vehicles, clattering less noisily than usual over its pine block roadway, laid to deaden the noise of traffic.

COLLEGE GREEN
1897 39212
Looking east over College Green to the main
facade of Trinity College. College Green was still
common land in the 17th century when Trinity
College was founded. Today it is a busy traffic
junction, and this old view appears uncluttered
and almost serene by comparison.

TRINITY COLLEGE AND BANK 1897 39210
Looking north round College Green into Westmoreland Street, which is busy with pedestrians and horse drawn vehicles. The main facade of Trinity College stands on the right with its statues by Foley of famous alumni Edmund Burke and Oliver Goldsmith, while on the left is the Bank of Ireland.

THE CUSTOM HOUSE 1897 39222
The Custom House dates from 1791 but was burned down in 1921 during the troubled years that led to the creation of the Irish Free State. The extensive damage was not completely made good until 1991. It now houses government offices, while Custom House Docks, originally developed at the same time as the Custom House, are now a financial services centre.

THE RIVER LIFFEY, THE NORTH WALL 1897 39282
The North Wall was the first part of Dublin Harbour to be developed. A busy North Wall Quay and the River Liffey are pictured here, with warehouses visible on the right and both steam and sailing vessels moored at the quayside.

THE RIVER LIFFEY 1897 39283
The busy port on the River Liffey, showing several steamers with smoking funnels waiting to depart and, on the right, a forest of masts of sailing ships.

PHOENIX PARK 1897 39271
A view along Chesterfield Avenue, the main drive through Phoenix Park . The park is the largest urban park in Europe, five times the size of London's Hyde Park. The land it encloses was turned into a deer park by the Duke of Ormonde in 1662 and later landscaped and opened to the public by Lord Chesterfield in the 1740s.

ST STEPHEN'S GREEN, THE CASCADE 1897 39219
St Stephen's Green on the south of the city was one of the three ancient commons enclosed in 1663. It covers 22 acres and was laid out as a park in 1880 with a lake and other water features.

THE SHELBOURNE HOTEL 39216
A view along St Stephen's Green North, showing
hansom cabs and the famous Shelbourne Hotel
when it was just thirty years old. This north side of
the green was known as Beaux Walk in the
19th century because of its numerous
gentlemen's clubs, several of which still exist.

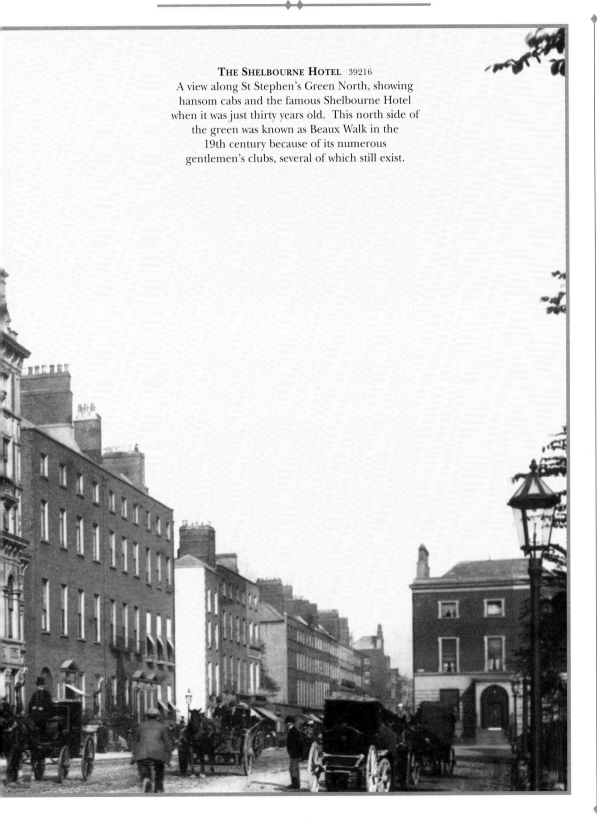

St Stephen's Green, The Lake and the College 39220

ST STEPHEN'S GREEN
The Lake and the College
Looking across the lake in St Stephen's Green to the portico of the Royal College of Surgeons. It was designed by Edward Parke in 1806 and completed in 1829. During the Easter Rising of 1916 it was captured by the insurgents led by Constance Markievicz, and it still bears bullet marks on its columns.

◆

TERENURE
c1900
Dublin had an extensive tramway system, the oldest route from College Green to Garville Avenue dating from 1872. The route was later incorporated into the Nelson's Pillar to Terenure route, and this is a picture of a tram at the Terenure terminus.

TERENURE c1900 D58001

The City's Buildings

THE GRANDEUR of much of Dublin's architecture is well known, in particular its handsome Georgian buildings on wide well-planned streets and squares. These were erected during Dublin's first great period of affluence, when cultured, rich Dubliners determined to make their city the handsomest in Europe. This period of building, which peaked around 1783 when the Irish Parliament was granted autonomy from Westminster, came to an abrupt end with the Act of Union in 1800, which left Dublin a backwater. These photographs, dating from the 1890s, concentrate on the famous Georgian buildings including the Custom House and the Four Courts, and, to a lesser extent, on grand Victorian ones, such as the National Museum, which had been more recently erected.

The most famous architect of Georgian Dublin was James Gandon, who designed the Custom House, the Four Courts and the east portico of the Bank of Ireland, all of which are represented here, as well as the King's Inns. Gandon, an Englishman, turned down prestigious work in Russia to come to Ireland at Lord Beresford's invitation to design the Custom House in 1781. The Custom House took ten years to build and was fiercely opposed by some merchants, so that Gandon had to travel armed with a sword for fear of attack.

His next Dublin project, the Four Courts, was also dogged by intrigue and controversy. The building has a 450ft long frontage to the River Liffey and the figures above the Corinthian portico represent Moses flanked by Justice and Mercy. Both the Custom House and the Four Courts suffered heavy destruction during the Irish Civil War, but have since been restored.

One of Dublin's most splendid Georgian buildings is the Bank of Ireland on College Green. Originally built in 1739 as the Irish Parliament, it was the first purpose-built parliament house in Europe. The architect was Edward Lovett Pearce, Surveyor-General of Ireland. In 1785 James Gandon contributed to its development, adding the eastern portico which gives access to the House of Lords. After the Act of Union in 1800 the Bank of Ireland bought the building for £40,000 and completed it with the curving screen in 1808.

Dublin Castle, which lies at the historic core of the city, was originally built by the Anglo-Norman King John in 1205-08. It crowns Cork Hill, a defensible site above the River Liffey and its tributary the River Poddle. It was once the site of a Celtic rath and a Viking stronghold. It had to be substantially rebuilt after a disastrous fire in 1684 and the present castle, used for state functions, is much more of a palace than a stronghold. The most substantial fragment of the 13th century building is the Record Tower, but parts of the walls also survive.

Elizabeth I founded Trinity College in 1572 on the site of an Augustinian monastery, dissolved earlier that century. Sadly no Elizabethan buildings survive, though the Victorian photographer gives us a century-old view of the 'Rubrics', the earliest extant college buildings dating from about 1700, where Oliver Goldsmith once had chambers.

THE FOUR COURTS
1897 39224
A famous Dublin landmark, Cooley and Gandon's
magnificent Four Courts, built in 1785 and gutted by
fire in the Civil War of 1922. Restored, it opened
again for business in October 1931. The copper
covered lantern dome had to be completely rebuilt.

THE CUSTOM HOUSE 1897 39223

James Gandon's masterpiece, the Custom House, completed in 1791. The Custom House was gutted by fire during the Civil War. It was not fully restored until 1991, when the four figures over the portico facing the river were replaced at last by replicas.

THE CASTLE, THE STATE ENTRANCE 1897 39260

Dublin Castle remained the centre of British power in Ireland from King John's time onwards. The Norman castle burnt down in 1684 and little survives. It was replaced by the present castle - more of a palace - built around Upper and Lower Castle Yards. This picture shows Upper Yard and the Bedford Tower of 1760, and is little changed today.

THE BANK OF IRELAND 1897 39209

This magnificent building, unobscured by traffic or pedestrians in this photograph, was originally built by Edward Lovett Pearce in 1739 as the Irish Parliament. In 1785 James Gandon added the east entrance (on the right of the picture) giving access to the House of Lords.

THE ROTUNDA AND THE HOSPITAL 1897 39211

The Rotunda Hospital of 1757, the first purpose-built maternity hospital in Ireland or Britain, and the adjacent Rotunda of 1764. This tall hall, 80 feet in diameter, now houses a cinema, but was originally used as a venue for the hospital's fundraising events and functioned as an Assembly Hall in the 18th century. The Irish composer John Field gave his first public performance here, and Liszt also gave a concert.

TRINITY COLLEGE, THE QUADRANGLE 1897 39230
Trinity College was founded in 1592 by Elizabeth I, and this picture of the main quadrangle looks towards the oldest extant college buildings, the red brick 'Rubrics', of about 1700, where Oliver Goldsmith once had his chambers. The old library and Examination Hall are on the right. In the centre is the 98ft high bell tower of 1853.

TRINITY COLLEGE, THE LIBRARY 1897 39233

The famous Long Room of the old library. This 210ft long room houses about 200,000 antiquarian books. The room was altered in 1857, with first and second floors thrown together under a timber barrel-vaulted roof. It is a major tourist attraction and has changed but little since this picture was taken.

TRINITY COLLEGE, THE LIBRARY 1897 39234

A ground floor view of the Long Room showing the flanking busts of scholars. Famous students of Trinity include Oliver Goldsmith, Jonathan Swift, Edmund Burke, Oscar Wilde and Samuel Becket. Illuminated manuscripts, including the Book of Kells, are on display in the Colonade.

TRINITY COLLEGE, THE MEDICAL SCHOOL 1897 39236

This is one of many 19th century science buildings to the east of Trinity. Interestingly, Trinity was originally a Protestant college and Catholics were not admitted till the 1870s.

TRINITY COLLEGE, THE SCHOOL OF ENGINEERING 1897 39237
The School of Engineering is another of the science buildings east of College Park. Trinity College was very advanced in admitting female students to degrees as early as 1903, earlier than most universities.

THE NATIONAL MUSEUM 1897 39226
The National Museum photographed when it was only a few years old. The museum and its matching building, the National Library, were built in 1885-90 by Sir Thomas Deane.

THE SCHOOL OF ART
The Library 1897 39225
Leinster House, flanked by the National Library and
National Museum. Home of the Irish Parliament since
1922, the building was designed by Richard Cassels in
1745 for the Duke of Leinster.

THE NATURAL HISTORY MUSEUM 1897 39228

The Natural History Museum opened in 1857, with Dr David Livingston giving the inaugural lecture on African fauna. The museum has changed little today and houses a notable collection of stuffed animals, including the skeletons of two whales washed up on the Irish coast in Victorian times.

THE VICEREGAL LODGE FROM PHOENIX PARK 1897 39266

At this time, this Georgian building dating from 1751 was the home of the King's representative in Ireland, and is now 'Aras an Uachtarain', the Irish president's official residence. The building was enlarged in 1782 and in 1816 the Ionic portico was added by Francis Johnson.

THE VICEREGAL LODGE
1897

The Phoenix Park Murders, the murder by the 'Invincibles' of the Chief Secretary, Lord Frederick Cavendish, and the Under-Secretary, Thomas Burke, took place near here in broad daylight in May 1882.

◆

THE CHIEF SECRETARY'S LODGE
Phoenix Park 1897

A sunny summer's day outside the Chief Secretary's Lodge. This elegant Georgian house, enlarged in 1775 and later modified, is now 'Deerfield', home of the American Ambassador.

THE VICEREGAL LODGE 1897   39268

THE CHIEF SECRETARY'S LODGE, PHOENIX PARK 1897   39269

Cathedrals and Churches

THE HISTORY of Dublin's cathedrals and churches is fascinating. The island has a long history of Catholicism, which began with the early Celtic Catholic Church founded shortly after the collapse of Roman rule in the west. Later, the Celtic and the restablished Roman churches reunited, although not without bitter controversy, which included disagreements as to how the date of Easter should be calculated.

Ireland did not escape the break with Rome and the Dissolution of the Monasteries under Henry VIII. This led to the creation of the Church of Ireland which, unlike the Church of England, became disestablished in the late 19th century. From the time of the dissolution until the creation of the Irish Free State, the Church of Ireland was the dominant force in Irish religious affairs, although the majority of the people of the island remained Roman Catholic. Since partition, the Church of Ireland has struggled to survive in many parts of Ireland, but it has thrived in Dublin. This may be explained in part, perhaps, by Dublin's cosmopolitan nature when compared to the rest of Ireland.

Given this historic background, it is not surprising to find that the two cathedrals in Dublin, Christchurch and St Patrick's, both belong to the Anglican Communion. Both of these are believed to be founded on ancient Christian sites dating from Celtic times. Christchurch is the mother church, and was founded in 1038 by Donat, the first Bishop of Dublin. It was rebuilt in the 12th century under Bishop St Lawrence O'Toole.

St Patrick's dates from Anglo-Norman times, and was raised to Cathedral status by Comyn, the first Anglo-Norman Archbishop of Dublin.

A fierce rivalry developed between the two, which was settled by a Papal decree in favour of Christchurch in 1300. Both cathedrals were in a poor state in early Victorian times, but both were rebuilt to the fine buildings of today.

There are also some fine old parish churches, many of which also date back to Celtic times. One of the best known is St Michan, a small church near the Four Courts. It is well-known for its 'mummified' corpses found in the crypt. It also has an organ that is reputed to have been played on by Handel. The former Parish Church of Dublin, St Werburgh's, was rebuilt in 1784. It was here that the Viceroy was sworn in. It has a pulpit thought to be carved by Grindling Gibbons. Other fine churches from the early 19th century include St Francis Xavier, which has an Ionic Portico, and St George's, a notable church dating from 1802 with a spire 200ft tall.

The principal catholic church, St Mary's, has never been raised formally to cathedral status, but has been known for over a century as the 'Pro-cathedral'. It was built in Greek revival style and has a fine interior and magnificent dome. The building is attributed to Sweetman, who was in exile after the 1798 rebellion, but the architect may have been Louis Hippolyte le Bas, one of Napoleon's architects. The three statues on the top are St Lawrence O'Toole (the 12th century archbishop of Dublin), St Mary and St Patrick. John, later Cardinal, Newman, made his profession of faith here in 1851.

Two of Dublin's famous institutions, Trinity College and Dublin Castle, also have wonderful chapels, and these were also recorded faithfully by the photographer.

CHRISTCHURCH CATHEDRAL 1897 39254
Christchurch Cathedral and the former Synod Hall (now Dublinia). The cathedral was renovated in the 1870s, when its partly ruinous fabric was restored by Henry Roe, who also built the Synod Hall (on the left) and connecting bridge. The building dates from the 12th century. It was commissioned in 1172 by Strongbow and Archbishop Lawrence O'Toole to replace the wooden Viking church of 1038. It passed to the Church of Ireland at the Reformation.

CHRISTCHURCH CATHEDRAL, THE NAVE 1897 39257
A magnificent view of the 68ft high nave at Christchurch. On the north side the walls are about two feet out of true because of subsidence and the collapse of the south walls in 1569. The nave dates from about 1230, and is the work of English masons of the school of Glastonbury.

CHRISTCHURCH CATHEDRAL
The Nave 1897
A further view of the magnificent nave, this time looking west to where view number 39257 was taken. The cathedral has witnessed many historic events, not least the coronation of Lambert Simnel in 1487, supported by the Archbishop of Dublin and the Lord Deputy.

◆

CHRISTCHURCH CATHEDRAL
The Nave 1897
A final view of Christchurch, again looking east along the nave. The massive nature of the architecture is clearly seen. The fine vaulted roof is clearly visible, as is the leaning north wall of the nave, sloping outward as it rises.

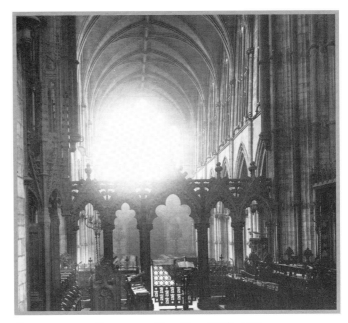

CHRISTCHURCH CATHEDRAL, THE NAVE 1897 39258

CHRISTCHURCH CATHEDRAL, THE NAVE 1897 39256

CHRISTCHURCH CATHEDRAL 1897 39255

A close-up showing the foundations of the original Chapter House dating back to the early 18th century. On the right can be seen the Romanesque doorway leading to the South Transept, a very fine example of 12th century stonework. The building in the middle distance is the Synod Hall, now Dublinia.

ST PATRICK'S CATHEDRAL, FROM THE SOUTH EAST 1897 39243

St Patrick's is about 400 yards from Christchurch. It is the largest church in Ireland, with a 143ft tower (Minot's tower) of 1370. The 100ft spire was added in the 17th century by George Simple. The church was restored in 1864-69 by Sir Benjamin Lee Guinness. The site is said to be that of a Celtic Church of around 450AD, where St Patrick baptised converts. In 1901, a well was discovered in the grounds. Today it is the 'National Cathedral' of the Church of Ireland.

ST PATRICK'S CATHEDRAL, THE NAVE 1897 39248
The choir and the nave, looking west. The clear tradition with the English cathedrals is apparent in the richly carved choir stalls and the regalia. This is the best preserved part of the medieval cathedral. It was formerly the Chapel of the Order of St Patrick, which was moved to Dublin Castle after the disestablishment of the Church of Ireland. The Order was founded by George III in 1783, and the Knights' banners hang above the stalls.

ST PATRICK'S CATHEDRAL, THE CHOIR 1897 39247

A magnificent view, looking east along the choir to the High Altar and the east window. The photographer has emphasised the massive proportions of the cathedral, with its high vaulted roof and finely decorated stonework. The elaborate pulpit and the Knights' banners dominate the view.

ST PATRICK'S CATHEDRAL, THE NAVE 1897 39245

A view taken from the west entrance, looking straight down the nave to the east window. St Patrick's is the largest church in Ireland, and this picture demonstrates its spacious proportions. The total length of the cathedral is about 300ft. It fell into disrepair during the 17th and 18th centuries and the piers of the nave arcade had to be rebuilt.

ST PATRICK'S CATHEDRAL, THE NAVE 1897 39249

Another fine study, this time looking west along the nave to the west front. The flags shown in the previous picture are seen near the Gate. This view is taken from near the choir and pulpit.

ST PATRICK'S CATHEDRAL, THE LADY CHAPEL 1897 39250

The square-ended eastern Lady Chapel, similar to the one at Salisbury Cathedral, was built in 1270. When the Huguenots arrived from France, the Dean and Chapter gave them the Lady Chapel as their place of worship - it was separated from the rest of the cathedral and remained in their use until the 18th century. It suffered badly from neglect and became a complete ruin, but was rebuilt in 1845-50 by Richard Carpenter.

ST PATRICK'S CATHEDRAL, DEAN SWIFT'S TABLET 1897 39252
Swift (1667 - 1745), became Dean of St Patrick's in 1713. He was probably the greatest satirist in the English language and Swift memorabilia are preserved in the west transept, now known as Swift's Corner. It includes an altar table and bookcase with his death mask.

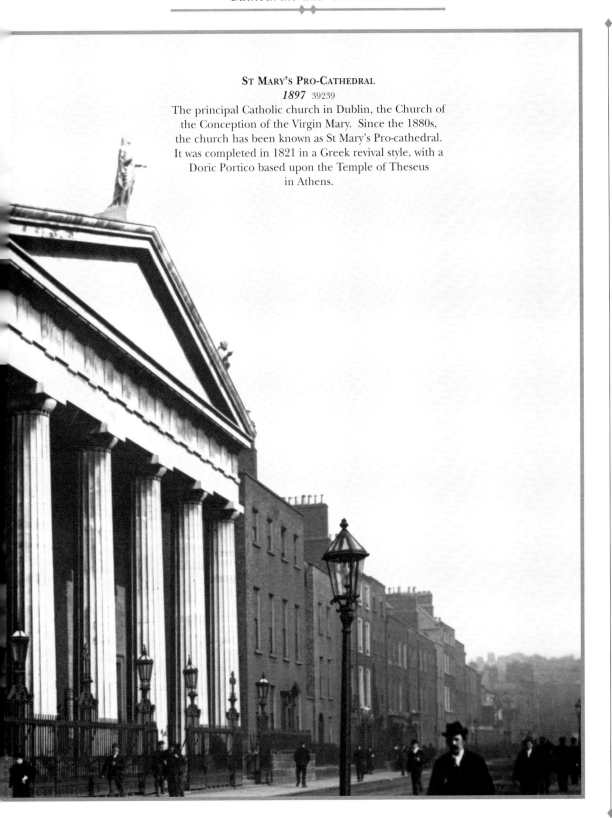

ST MARY'S PRO-CATHEDRAL
1897 39239
The principal Catholic church in Dublin, the Church of
the Conception of the Virgin Mary. Since the 1880s,
the church has been known as St Mary's Pro-cathedral.
It was completed in 1821 in a Greek revival style, with a
Doric Portico based upon the Temple of Theseus
in Athens.

THE ROMAN CATHOLIC CATHEDRAL 1897 39241

THE ROMAN CATHOLIC CATHEDRAL 1897 39240

THE ROMAN CATHOLIC CATHEDRAL
1897
A fine view of the magnificent Neo-classical interior of the Pro-cathedral, showing the nave and aisles with heavy Doric pillars. The aisles have been extended since this picture was taken. The Palestrina Choir was endowed in 1902 by Edward Mostyn (who with Lady Gregory founded the Abbey Theatre). John McCormack, the famous Irish tenor, was a member of the choir in those early years.

◆

THE ROMAN CATHOLIC CATHEDRAL
1897
A final view of the Pro-cathedral, showing the stucco of the Ascension, and the massive dome. The intricately carved High Altar is by Peter Turnerelle (1774 - 1839), who was from Belfast.

THE CHAPEL ROYAL 1890 24580

THE CHAPEL ROYAL
1890

The imposing Chapel Royal at Dublin Castle. It was completed in 1814 by Francis Johnson, and is situated in the Lower Yard, on the site of an earlier, smaller, chapel. In the background is the Record Tower, which dates from 1258. The one hundred heads on the exterior are carved by Edward Smyth. It is now known as the Church of the Most Holy Trinity.

◆

THE CHAPEL ROYAL
Interior 1897

The interior plasterwork is by George Stapleton, with woodwork by Richard Steward. The Arms of all the Viceroys from 1172 to 1922 are carved on the woodwork of the galleries and chancel, and are also pictured in stained glass in the gallery windows. The east window shows scenes from the Passion using old stained glass from Europe.

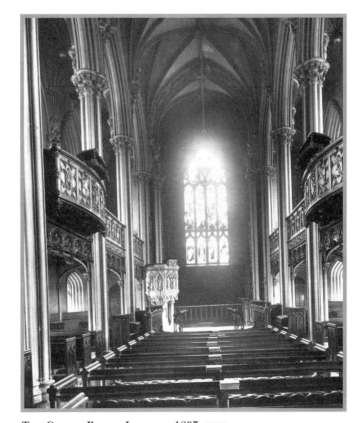

THE CHAPEL ROYAL, INTERIOR 1897 39263

TRINITY COLLEGE CHAPEL, INTERIOR LOOKING WEST 1897 39232

Today, this is the only interdenominational chapel in the Republic of Ireland. It was designed by Sir William Chambers (1723-96) in the 1790s, and is on the site of the early medieval monastic church of All Hallows. The stucco is again by Michael Stapleton. The organ case dates from the 18th century.

TRINITY COLLEGE CHAPEL, INTERIOR LOOKING EAST 1897 39231

Looking east towards the Altar. The painted windows date from 1867, and the main window is dedicated to Archbishop Ussher.

St Michan's Church, Interior 1890 24581
The church was built in 1686 on the site of an 11th century church. The original church was probably built by the Danes, and St Michan is likely to have been a Danish saint. The organ, which dates from 1724, is said to have been played by Handel. On the panel directly beneath the organ can be seen the intricate wood carving of flutes and violins. Edmund Burke was baptised here, and Robert Emmett is said to be buried in the churchyard.

Monuments and Memorials

DUBLIN is a city filled with monuments: statues, plaques, obelisks and portrait busts seem to spring up along every street and in every park. Wherever you go in Dublin you are reminded of the past, and of the people who once walked her streets. This is in part at least a reflection of the fact that many remarkable people have been associated with Dublin and that Dublin likes to advertise the fact. Since the Victorian photographer captured a few of these monuments in the late 1890s, many more have been added - including monuments to the patriots of the 1916 Easter Rising and to such great literary figures as Yeats, Joyce and Bernard Shaw. A fair number have vanished, bombed or discreetly removed as symbols of British oppression.

The monument to Daniel O'Connell in O'Connell Street is probably the most famous Dublin statue. Like several others in the city it was executed by John Henry Foley. Erected in 1854, it shows the famous lawyer who fought for Catholic Emancipation and became Dublin's first Catholic Lord Mayor in thoughtful contemplation. The four winged victories around the base are a later addition of 1882, executed by Thomas Brock eight years after Foley's death. They represent Patriotism, Fidelity, Eloquence and Courage - O'Connell's particular virtues. The other monuments by Foley included here are his fine likeness of Henry Grattan, who won legislative independence for Ireland in 1782 which enabled the repeal of some of the crippling anti-Catholic laws, and his monument to Prince Albert.

The Wellington Monument in Phoenix Park, Robert Smirke's big obelisk - the tallest in the world when designed in 1817 - was completed in 1861. It commemorates Arthur Wellesley, Duke of Wellington, victor over Napoleon at Waterloo in 1815, who was born and attended school in Dublin. Wellington's memorial has survived the bombs, unlike the equestrian statue of Field Marshal Gough which used to stand in Phoenix Park. Hugh, Viscount Gough (1779 - 1869) was also an Irishman, a distinguished soldier, born in Limerick and descended from a famous Irish bishop. He served under Wellington in the Peninsula War and rose to the position of Field Marshal.

No collection of Victorian photographs would be complete without a glimpse of the era's grandiose cemetery memorials, and Frith's photographer sought out the famous graves at Glasnevin Cemetery. Glasnevin, properly called Prospect Cemetery, is the principal burial ground in Dublin and dates from 1831 when Daniel O'Connell organised the use of nine acres of land for Catholic burials. It is now the largest cemetery in Ireland, covering 120 acres, and the last resting place of over one million people. A list of those interred here reads like a biographical index to modern Ireland: Daniel O'Connell, Charles Stewart Parnell, Michael Collins, Sir Roger Casement, Maud Gonne, Eamon de Valera and numerous others. These 1890s pictures are remarkable for showing so many of the older graves when they were relatively new.

THE O'CONNELL STATUE 1897 39208
The famous statue of Daniel O'Connell (1775 - 1847), the 'Liberator', which stands at the foot of O'Connell (in those days, Sackville) Street. The monument is by John Foley and the foundation stone was laid in 1854.

THE GRATTAN STATUE 1897 39213
This statue of Henry Grattan (1746 - 1820) stands outside the Bank of Ireland (formerly the Parliament House) and shows the great orator in the act of speaking. The statue is by John Foley and was unveiled in 1879.

THE WELLINGTON MONUMENT, PHOENIX PARK 1899 24569
This 204ft (63m) high obelisk on the south side of the main road was designed by Robert Smirke and believed to be the highest in the world at the time. The obelisk was begun in 1817 and completed in 1861. The bas relief in bronze is made from captured French cannons.

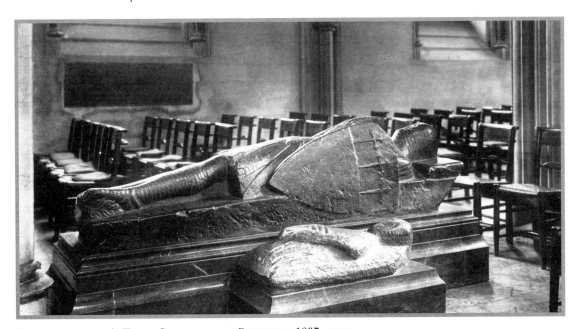

EARL OF PEMBROKE'S TOMB, CHRISTCHURCH CATHEDRAL 1897 39259
The famous Strongbow Monument. It commemorates Richard de Clare, Earl of Pembroke, who initiated the building of the cathedral and died in 1176. It is probable that the curious half figure is the original tomb effigy. The full-length figure (which bears the arms of FitzOsbert of Drogheda) is probably a replacement procured by the Lord Deputy, Sir Henry Sidney, when the original effigy was broken when the south nave wall collapsed in 1569.

THE GEORGE II STATUE
St Stephen's Green 1897 39218
The former statue of George II which used to stand
on St Stephen's Green. Regarded as symbolic of
British oppression, the statue was bombed
away in 1937.

THE GOUGH MONUMENT 1897 39273
The now vanished Gough Monument, which used to stand in Phoenix Park. The statue's head and sword arm were sawn off in 1944 and the mutilated remains were bombed twice, in 1956 and 1957.

THE ALBERT STATUE 1897 39229
The statue of Prince Albert by John Foley. This monument has survived the changes in Ireland since its unveiling. It stands on Leinster Lawn beside Leinster House, home of the Irish Parliament.

CURRAN'S TOMB, GLASNEVIN CEMETERY 1897 39280
John Philpott Curran (1750 - 1817), the great Irish judge and orator, was a staunch supporter of Henry Grattan and father of Sarah, luckless girlfriend of the patriot Robert Emmett. Curran, though a convinced Protestant, was a tireless supporter of oppressed Catholics. He strove to try to save the leaders of the 1798 Rebellion.

O'CONNELL'S TOMB, GLASNEVIN CEMETERY 1897 39275
This modern replica of an Irish round tower was built in 1869 to mark the tomb of Daniel O'Connell in Glasnevin Cemetery. O'Connell had died in 1847 but was reinterred here in 1869, though his heart is buried in Rome.

BARRY SULLIVAN'S GRAVE, GLASNEVIN CEMETERY 1897 39278

Barry (Thomas) Sullivan (1821 - 91) was a celebrated Irish actor, particularly of Shakespearean parts, who became well-known worldwide. He made his first London appearance as Hamlet in 1852 and toured America and Australia.

PARNELL'S GRAVE, GLASNEVIN CEMETERY 1897 39276
The grave of Charles Stewart Parnell (1846 - 91). Parnell was a great Irish patriot, a Protestant landowner from Wicklow and MP at Westminster, whose career was ruined by scandal following the disclosure of his long-term affair with a married woman, Kitty O'Shea.

PARNELL'S GRAVE, GLASNEVIN CEMETERY 1897 39277
Parnell had wholeheartedly espoused the causes of the Land League and Home Rule, doing much to improve the lot of his impoverished compatriots. As was his wish, Parnell was buried in a mass grave among the people of Ireland whom he loved. His name is carved on a large boulder.

HONEST TOM STEELE'S MONUMENT, GLASNEVIN CEMETERY 1897 39281
Honest Tom Steele's monument is near the entrance of the cemetery. Many of the tombs carry shamrock, Irish harp and wolfhound motifs, indicative of the Young Ireland Movement.

GLASNEVIN CEMETERY 1897 39279
Monuments and obelisks among the trees of Glasnevin Cemetery. There is a very classical style to the tombs in this corner of the cemetery.

HOWTH
General View 1897 39284
A panorama looking north over the town to Ireland's Eye.
The island forms a natural breakwater to the harbour.
The Martello tower is visible on the headland to the left.

Howth

HOWTH HEAD is a rock promontory situated at the north side of Dublin Bay. It is separated from the mainland by a sandy bar, and is less than two miles across. The Head is famous for its rocky moorland scenery, as well as its wonderful views north to the Mourne Mountains and south to the Wicklow hills. The highest point of the Head, Ben of Howth, rises to about 563ft. The only town, Howth, is situated on the north side of the Head, and is about 9 miles from Dublin. Much of the interior of the Head is now taken up with golf courses. Howth has been very much a well-to-do suburb of Dublin for many years, and is at the terminus of a suburban line that is today electrified.

Howth was also known for its tramway. This was a tramway built to the standard Irish gauge of 5ft 3in, and which connected the town, via the Hill of Howth, with the village of Sutton on the west end of the Head. Famous in its day, not least for its open tramcars, the tramway closed in 1959, although some of the trams are now preserved elsewhere.

Although it is today very much a suburban town, Howth has an interesting history, both as an historic site and also as a port. St Lawrence was granted the manor and settled here in 1180, and his castle stood on the site of the Martello tower standing above the harbour that can be seen on these photos.

A new harbour was built at Howth by Rennie at the beginning of the 19th century, and was the terminus of the Irish Sea mail boats to Holyhead. However, the harbour suffered from silting, and the decision was taken to build a new harbour at Dun Laoghaire, situated on the south side of Dublin Bay. The vast new harbour there was also laid out by Rennie, and once that was completed, the old port of Howth slipped into obscurity. It became the home of the Howth fishing fleet, and also yacht clubs, and was the scene of arms smuggling prior to the rising in 1916.

About a mile to the north of Howth is an island known as Ireland's Eye which, like many islands of Ireland, has a history which stretches back to the dawn of the Celtic Church. There are still traces of the original foundation on the island, which can be visited by boat. The later church and abbey was removed to Howth and built above what is now the harbour. However, this too has been ruinous for many years.

Near to the harbour can be found the great Howth Castle, which has been the seat of the Lawrence family since the 16th century. It has been rebuilt, modernised, and enlarged over the years. In this century, Lutyens was the architect responsible for the modernisation. Legend has it that Howth Castle must never be closed against the hungry traveller, and even today a place is always set at the St Lawrence table for the unexpected guest.

HOWTH, FROM ABOVE THE NEW CHAPEL 1897 39285

A similar view to the previous picture, but showing the harbour mouth and lighthouse and the coast stretching away to the north. Note the typical thatched Irish cottages. Yeats' family lived in Howth in a cottage overlooking the harbour about twenty years before this picture was taken.

HOWTH, THE CASTLE 1897 39304

A superb view of an ivy-decked Howth Castle. It dates from 1564, and is a rather long and irregular building, flanked by massive square towers, which are perhaps the remains of an older castle.

HOWTH, THE HEAD FROM THE TOWER 1897 39299

A view looking east from the tower towards the head. The large villas, signs of Howth's emerging prosperity as a commuter town to Dublin, are visible on the hillside.

HOWTH, THE HEAD 1897 39300

This view shows clearly the rocky promontory of the Head, which was known in Celtic times as Beann Eadir, or Eadar's peak. It is connected to the mainland and Dublin Bay by a sandy spit.

HOWTH, THE LADIES' BATHING BEACH 1897 39301
A view looking north west, past the tower and along the east wall of the harbour, to Ireland's Eye. The bathing huts of the Ladies' bathing beach can be clearly seen in the bottom left of the picture.

HOWTH, FROM THE EAST PIER 1897 39294
A marvellously evocative view looking to the town from the east pier. The Tower is on the hill to the left. In this glorious summer scene, boats are moored along the jetty. It is difficult to believe that less than twenty years later, the harbour was the scene of nationalist gun-running.

HOWTH, IRELAND'S EYE 1897 39302
A fine view looking around the sweeping east pier of Howth harbour to the lighthouse. In the distance, just under a mile away, is Ireland's Eye. The small rocky island has an excellent beach, together with the ruins of the 6th century St Nessan's Abbey.

HOWTH, THE ABBEY 1897 39286
Howth is well-known both for its harbour and its former Abbey church, now ruined. In this view, the prominent site of the Abbey, on a bluff overlooking the harbour, is clearly visible.

HOWTH, THE ABBEY
Tomb of the 13th Earl of Howth 1897

Howth Abbey church, although ruined for many years, contains a number of fine monuments. The best known is the tomb of the thirteenth Earl of Howth.

◆

HOWTH
The Abbey 1897

Howth Abbey is also known as the collegiate church of Saint Mary. It is believed to have been founded in 1235, although it is based upon a Viking foundation. This view shows the massive proportions of the west front.

HOWTH, THE ABBEY, TOMB OF THE 13TH EARL 1897 39290

HOWTH, THE ABBEY 1897 39289

HOWTH
The Abbey 1897 39287
The church was founded to take the place of St Nessan's, on
the nearby island of Ireland's Eye. The bells are preserved
in Howth Castle.

HOWTH, THE HARBOUR AND SEA FRONT 1897 39298

A peaceful view of Howth harbour, looking along the sea wall towards the tower and the east pier. Rowing boats are moored in the harbour. Following the transfer of the mail boat service to Dun Laoghaire, Howth harbour had by this time settled down to a quiet existence.

HOWTH, THE HARBOUR 1897 39292

The spacious harbour, with assorted fishing and sailing craft moored. It is hard to imagine that this tranquil harbour scene is only about nine miles away from the bustling, industrial scenes of Dublin Harbour seen earlier in this book.

HOWTH, FROM THE PIERHEAD 1897 39293
Howth harbour, looking from the west pier to the east harbour wall, with the promontory visible on the left. A beautifully proportioned schooner lies anchored just inside the harbour.

HOWTH
The Harbour 1897 39297
A close-up of rowing and fishing boats, drawn up on the
shore at low tide. The Martello tower is again visible in
the distance. The superb lines of the boats of the
Howth fishing fleet can be seen clearly.

Index

Frith Book Co 1999 Titles

From 2000 we aim at publishing 100 new books each year. For latest catalogue please contact Frith Book Co

Barnstaple	1-85937-084-5	£12.99	Oct 99		Maidstone	1-85937-056-X	£12.99	Sep 99
Blackpool	1-85937-049-7	£12.99	Sep 99		Northumberland & Tyne and Wear	1-85937-072-1	£14.99	Sep 99
Bognor Regis	1-85937-055-1	£12.99	Sep 99		North Yorkshire	1-85937-048-9	£14.99	Sep 99
Bristol	1-85937-050-0	£12.99	Sep 99		Nottingham	1-85937-060-8	£12.99	Sep 99
Cambridge	1-85937-092-6	£12.99	Oct 99		Oxfordshire	1-85937-076-4	£14.99	Oct 99
Cambridgeshire	1-85937-086-1	£14.99	Nov 99		Penzance	1-85937-069-1	£12.99	Sep 99
Cheshire	1-85937-045-4	£14.99	Sep 99		Reading	1-85937-087-X	£12.99	Nov 99
Chester	1-85937-090-X	£12.99	Nov 99		St Ives	1-85937-068-3	£12.99	Sep 99
Chesterfield	1-85937-071-3	£12.99	Sep 99		Salisbury	1-85937-091-8	£12.99	Nov 99
Chichester	1-85937-089-6	£12.99	Nov 99		Scarborough	1-85937-104-3	£12.99	Sep 99
Cornwall	1-85937-054-3	£14.99	Sep 99		Scottish Castles	1-85937-077-2	£14.99	Oct 99
Cotswolds	1-85937-099-3	£14.99	Nov 99		Sevenoaks and Tonbridge	1-85937-057-8	£12.99	Sep 99

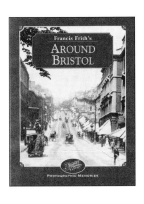
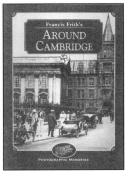

					Sheffield and S Yorkshire	1-85937-070-5	£12.99	Sep 99
					Shropshire	1-85937-083-7	£14.99	Nov 99
					Southampton	1-85937-088-8	£12.99	Nov 99
					Staffordshire	1-85937-047-0	£14.99	Sep 99
					Stratford upon Avon	1-85937-098-5	£12.99	Nov 99
					Suffolk	1-85937-074-8	£14.99	Oct 99
					Surrey	1-85937-081-0	£14.99	Oct 99
					Torbay	1-85937-063-2	£12.99	Sep 99
					Wiltshire	1-85937-053-5	£14.99	Sep 99

Derby	1-85937-046-2	£12.99	Sep 99
Devon	1-85937-052-7	£14.99	Sep 99
Dorset	1-85937-075-6	£14.99	Oct 99
Dorset Coast	1-85937-062-4	£14.99	Sep 99
Dublin	1-85937-058-6	£12.99	Sep 99
East Anglia	1-85937-059-4	£14.99	Sep 99
Eastbourne	1-85937-061-6	£12.99	Sep 99
English Castles	1-85937-078-0	£14.99	Oct 99
Essex	1-85937-082-9	£14.99	Nov 99
Falmouth	1-85937-066-7	£12.99	Sep 99
Hampshire	1-85937-064-0	£14.99	Sep 99
Hertfordshire	1-85937-079-9	£14.99	Nov 99
Isle of Man	1-85937-065-9	£14.99	Sep 99
Liverpool	1-85937-051-9	£12.99	Sep 99

British Life A Century Ago

246 x 189mm 144pp, hardback. Black and white Lavishly illustrated with photos from the turn of the century, and with extensive commentary. It offers a unique insight into the social history and heritage of bygone Britain.

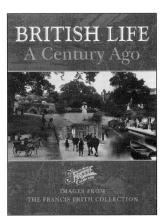

1-85937-103-5 £17.99 ....

Available from your local bookshop or from the publisher

FRITH PRODUCTS & SERVICES

Francis Frith would doubtless be pleased to know that the pioneering publishing venture he started in 1860 still continues today. More than a hundred and thirty years later, The Francis Frith Collection continues in the same innovative tradition and is now one of the foremost publishers of vintage photographs in the world. Some of the current activities include:

Interior Decoration

Today Frith's photographs can be seen framed and as giant wall murals in thousands of pubs, restaurants, hotels, banks, retail stores and other public buildings throughout the country. In every case they enhance the unique local atmosphere of the places they depict and provide reminders of gentler days in an increasingly busy and frenetic world.

Product Promotions

Frith products have been used by many major companies to promote the sales of their own products or to reinforce their own history and heritage. Brands include Hovis bread, Courage beers, Scots Porage Oats, Colman's mustard, Cadbury's foods, Mellow Birds coffee, Dunhill pipe tobacco, Guinness, and Bulmer's Cider.

Genealogy and Family History

As the interest in family history and roots grows world-wide, more and more people are turning to Frith's photographs of Great Britain for images of the towns, villages and streets where their ancestors lived; and, of course, photographs of the churches and chapels where their ancestors were christened, married and buried are an essential part of every genealogy tree and family album.

A series of easy-to-use CD Roms is planned for publication, and an increasing number of Frith photographs will be able to be viewed on specialist genealogy sites. A growing range of Frith books will be available on CD.

The Internet

Already thousands of Frith photographs can be viewed and purchased on the internet. By the end of the year 2000 some 60,000 Frith photographs will be available on the internet. The number of sites is constantly expanding, each focussing on different products and services from the Collection.
Some of the sites are listed below.

www.townpages.co.uk
www.familystorehouse.com
www.britannia.com
www.icollector.com
www.barclaysquare.co.uk
www.cornwall-online.co.uk

For background information on the Collection look at the two following sites:

www.francisfrith.com
www.francisfrith.co.uk

Frith Products

All Frith photographs are available Framed or just as Mounted Prints, and can be ordered from the address below. From time to time other products - Address Books, Calendars, Table Mats, Postcards etc - are available.

The Frith Collectors' Guild

In response to the many customers who enjoy collecting Frith photographs we have created the Frith Collectors' Guild. Members are entitled to a range of benefits, including a regular magazine, special discounts and special limited edition products.

For further information: if you would like further information on any of the above aspects of the Frith business please contact us at the address below:
The Francis Frith Collection, Frith's Barn, Teffont, Salisbury, Wiltshire England SP3 5QP.
Tel: +44 (0) 1722 716 376 Fax: +44 (0) 1722 716 881   Email: frithbook.co.uk

To receive your FREE Mounted Print

Cut out this Voucher and return it with your remittance for £1.50 to cover postage and handling. Choose any photograph included in this book. Your SEPIA print will be A4 in size, and mounted in a cream mount with burgundy rule lines, overall size 14 x 11 inches.

Order additional Mounted Prints at HALF PRICE (only £7.49 each*)

If there are further pictures you would like to order, possibly as gifts for friends and family, acquire them at half price (no additional postage and handling required).

Have your Mounted Prints framed*

For an additional £14.95 per print you can have your chosen Mounted Print framed in an elegant polished wood and gilt moulding, overall size 16 x 13 inches (no additional postage and handling required).

---

* IMPORTANT!
These special prices are only available if ordered using the original voucher on this page (no copies permitted) and at the same time as your free Mounted Print, for delivery to the same address

---

Voucher for FREE and Reduced Price Frith Prints

Picture no.	Page number	Qty	Mounted @ £7.49	Framed + £14.95	Total Cost
		1	Free of charge*	£	£
			£	£	£
			£	£	£
			£	£	£
			£	£	£
			£	£	£
			* Post & handling		£1.50
			Total Order Cost		£

Title: AROUND DUBLIN
058-6

Please do not photocopy this voucher. Only the original is valid, so please cut it out and return it to us.

I enclose a cheque / postal order for £ . . . .
made payable to 'The Francis Frith Collection'
OR please debit my Mastercard / Visa / Switch / Amex card

Number . . . .

Expires . . . .   Signature . . . .

Name Mr/Mrs/Ms . . . .

Address . . . .

. . . .

. . . .

. . . .

. . . . Postcode . . . .

Daytime Tel No . . . .   Valid to 31/12/01

Frith Collectors' Guild

From time to time we publish a magazine of news and stories about Frith photographs and further special offers of Frith products. If you would like 12 months FREE membership, please return this form and we will send you a New Member Pack.

Send completed forms to:
The Francis Frith Collection,
Frith's Barn, Teffont, Salisbury,
Wiltshire SP3 5QP

The Francis Frith Collectors' Guild

I would like to receive the New Members Pack offering 12 months FREE membership.

058-6

Name Mr/Mrs/Ms . . . .

Address . . . .

. . . .

. . . .

. . . . Postcode . . . .